Praise for

"With his trademark [...] sense of humor, Bill [...] exchange of letters between a mother and her son's teachers, nary a finger is wagged, nor a line drawn in the sand. Harley's keen understanding of the promise and possibility of clear and careful communication should be a lesson to us all. I laughed out loud, rubbed the goose bumps off my arms, and nodded respectfully in recognition of the strength of Bill Harley's creativity."
　— *Claire Green,* PRESIDENT, PARENTS' CHOICE FOUNDATION

"Bill Harley's insights into human nature ring true. From my work in the parenting field and as a mom of three, 'Between Home *and* School' offers comfort to parents that they – and their child – *will* survive the challenges of growing up. By deftly illuminating the strengths and weaknesses of parents, teachers and children as they interrelate, Harley's dialogue draws readers into a story that prompts thoughtful reflection about the value and potential of the teacher-student-parent relationship in shaping a child's life."
　— *Barbara Smith Decker,* NATIONAL PARENTING PUBLICATIONS AWARD (NAPPA) MANAGER

"Bill Harley's been in the school trenches for years, and it shows. He knows the secret to student success – the one that few people ever admit: it's as much about parent teacher communication as it is about genes or hard work."
　— *Danielle Wood,* EDITOR-IN-CHIEF, EDUCATION.COM

"A lyrical evocation of the parent-teacher dialogue that intimately describes how we can nurture our children during the tender years of their growing up. Tyler's story shows how parents and teachers can bridge the home-school divide. Absolutely touching and true."
　— *Renee Rose Shield, PhD,* PARENT OF 4, TEACHER OF MANY; CLINICAL ASSOCIATE PROFESSOR OF COMMUNITY HEALTH, BROWN UNIVERSITY

"This book absolutely nails the parent/teacher relationship and how it can work for or against a child, parent or teacher. Bill Harley's songs and stories have always made me want to be a better parent and a better citizen of the world and I love that he has turned his gift for observation and story into this wonderful parable."
　— *Sharon Levin,* CHILDREN'S LITERATURE REVIEWER AND CONSULTANT

"Bill Harley simply 'gets it' when it comes to not-perfect schools and not-perfect parents and not-perfect kids. If more of us from all sides of the home and school divide would approach things with Bill's perspective, our kids would be the big winners. *Between Home and School* provides a simple and beautiful example of a Mom and her son's teachers collaborating for long-term school success."
— *Tim Sullivan*, FOUNDER, SCHOOL FAMILY MEDIA AND PTO TODAY

"Once again Bill has captured the essence of very complicated relationships. He does it with humor and a deep understanding. I laughed. I cried. I related as a Mom. I took notice as a teaching professional. When I share this book with staff it will serve as an important reminder to pay close attention to the fragility of the human condition."
— *Suzanne C. Mills-Shaw*, LOWER SCHOOL ACADEMIC HEAD, PAUL CUFFEE SCHOOL, PROVIDENCE RI

"As both a teacher and a parent, this book gave me cause to reflect on the power of the communication that happens between school and home. With humor and truth, Bill gently reminds us to see each child as an individual – a unique person with strengths and weaknesses, hopes and fears, at turns experiencing great happiness and tremendous sorrow. He shows us that by keeping an open and honest line of communication on both ends, every child can experience success in school and in life."
— *Lynn M. Jeka*, CLASSROOM TEACHER AND SCHOOL IMPROVEMENT TEAM MEMBER, YERINGTON ELEMENTARY SCHOOL, YERINGTON NV

"*Between Home and School* tells the story of Tyler, and his journey from kindergarten to high school graduation with eloquence and simplicity. A testament to teachers and parents the book affirms the power of communication to make the difference between student success or falling between the cracks. But the ultimate joy of this book is that it will make you smile, laugh, cry, get angry, and cheer, as I did."
— *Barbara Walhberg*, PARENT, ENGLISH TEACHER, CRANSTON RI HIGH SCHOOL AND BOARD MEMBER, NEATE- NEW ENGLAND ASSOCIATION OF TEACHERS OF ENGLISH

"*Between Home and School* addresses the doubts and fears of parents and teachers with compassion, purpose and whimsy: home affects school affects home. There is a person and a life behind the roles of parent, student and teacher. Harley's observations are 'spot on.'"
— *Greg Weiss*, DRAMA & SPEECH TEACHER, JAMES HART & MILLENNIUM SCHOOLS (GRADES 5 - 8), HOMEWOOD, IL; STORYTELLER; AUTHOR

Between Home
and School

Letters,
Notes
and Emails

by BILL HARLEY

ROUND RIVER PRODUCTIONS
Seekonk, Massachusetts

©2010 by Bill Harley
All Rights Reserved
This book, or parts thereof, may not be reproduced in any form without prior written permission from the publisher. Please do not participate in or encourage piracy of copyrighted materials.

ROUND RIVER PRODUCTIONS
301 Jacob Street
Seekonk, MA 02771
http://www.billharley.com/betweenhomeandschool.asp
800-682-9522

ISBN 978-1-878126-56-6

To David Bourns
A steady hand and a great educator

Foreword

I talked with my sons' teachers everyday; it was an occupational hazard as I was the principal in their high school. And the most difficult of those conversations were about the boys.

They both did fine in school, so every conversation should have been good. But something about the dynamics of my one child in their class of twenty just made it tricky.

Sometimes I fretted too much; as when my wife and my oldest son's kindergarten/first grade teacher said it really was fine that he hid under the table during reading lessons. Other times I did not know how to intervene, or even if I should, when my younger son told stories about wasted time watching movies in health class.

School is what I do, and yet there I was, befuddled over what to say or not to say in order to help the guys navigate their education.

Bill Harley neatly captures the challenge of parent/teacher communication through the story he tells of one parent and the notes to and from school about her son, Tyler. More importantly, he teaches us a lesson about how to do it well, on both sides.

Tyler's mother works hard to find the right tone, ask the right questions, and has a sense of humor that you know is reflected in the actions of her son. She is anxious (aren't we all) but not pushy; demanding, but not demeaning.

Tyler's teachers, the ones we meet, respond to her the way every parent deserves—with patience, and with the knowledge that words matter and will be remembered. We see the very best of the teacher's craft in these notes home, from understanding child development to the challenges of adolescence.

Of course there are other teachers we do not meet. Harley has wisely chosen not to fill these pages with the letters that did not communicate or the lessons not well taught. In this age of 'teacher-bashing' it is refreshing to be reminded that most teachers care deeply and try to do the right thing by their students and families. With the pressures teachers and parents feel as test scores take priority over learning, it is sometimes hard to remember that it is the give and take of healthy, honest, and caring human dynamics that will best serve our children. I believe we learn the most from such models we should follow, rather than by being hectored over failures not to be repeated.

Tyler, our fictional student, is lucky. A mother who cares but does not hover and teachers who wait him out, confident in the adult he will become while enjoying the child that he is.

And we are lucky that yet again Bill Harley has found a story that shows us how good we can be, if we just let it happen.

George Wood
PRINCIPAL, FEDERAL HOCKING MIDDLE AND HIGH SCHOOLS, STEWART, OH
AUTHOR, *TIME TO LEARN: HOW TO CREATE HIGH SCHOOLS THAT SERVE ALL STUDENTS*

Introduction

In September of 1998 I got a call from the Rhode Island Foundation, asking me to tell stories to teachers at a conference. Specifically, they wanted me to tell stories about the connection between home and school. I agreed, even though I wasn't sure what stories I would tell. I didn't worry about it because, as a storyteller, many of my stories are about my experiences in school. As the date got closer, I panicked when I realized I had nothing to fit the bill.

Searching for a theme, I wrote down what I knew about the relationship between parents and teachers. I wrote as a parent of two boys, and as a performer who often works and talks with teachers. My notes included these observations:

- Teachers and parents are often scared of each other.
- Parents have memories of school, which they bring to any relationship with their child's teacher - this can help or hinder the relationship.
- Some parents don't seem to care.
- Some teachers don't seem to care.
- It's hard to point out failings to parents.
- It's hard to point out failings to teachers.
- There are some things that are beyond a teacher.
- There are some things that are beyond a parent.
- If they are both doing their jobs, they have the same goals.
- Together they can influence and direct a child to become the best person that child might be.

With these thoughts in mind, I wrote the letters that follow. It wasn't storytelling, but the letters tell the story, through quick snapshots, of a student's path from Kindergarten to high school graduation. Since then, I've read them at workshops and conferences around the country – they seem to strike a chord everywhere I go. This year, my wife Debbie Block insisted we put them in book form – she, our office manager Michele Eaton, and our designer Alison Tolman-Rogers have put more time into working on this book than I did in the initial writing. They deserve a large amount of the credit.

The letters reflect what is, by and large, a healthy relationship between parent and teacher. There are rough spots, because rough spots are part of life. While there are many, many horror stories about what happens when education and parenting fails, we benefit more when we envision what might be. These letters are what might be.

— Bill Harley

Between Home
and School

To the Kindergarten teacher, Miss Considine

Rhonda Bennet

Dear Miss Considine –

Tyler has been complaining every day that he does not have enough time to play outside with the other children. He says that he always gets outside last and feels left out. Is there some reason for this? Can you do anything about it? Please let me know what we can do.

By the way, he loves all the frogs you have on your desk.

Sincerely yours,

Rhonda Bennet

From the Kindergarten teacher

Dear Mrs. Bennet,

    Thank you for your note. You are right — Tyler often does not have enough time to play. There are a dozen children in my class who do not know how to zip their jackets and at least that many who cannot put their boots on. By the time I get the last one ready for recess, it is almost time to come in. Some people think I teach children, but what I really do is dress them! If you could work with Tyler on tying his shoes and zipping his jacket it would be a big help. I realize these don't sound like very big things, but I'm sure you know they are. Independence is more important to a five-year-old than to anyone else.

    By the way — I understand from Tyler that your husband has written some children's books. Would he like to come in some day and talk to the class?

                Sincerely yours,

                  Ellen Considine

To the Kindergarten teacher

Rhonda Bennet

Dear Ellen,

    Tyler is having trouble with the shoe-tying. I'm having him wear velcro for the time being, while we work on the knots.
    My husband is not a children's writer — he writes about children; the kids would think he's boring. Even he says so.

Yours,

Rhonda

From the first-grade teacher, Althea Elliot

From the desk of **Althea Elliot**

Dear Mrs. Bennet,

    Thank you for your call the other day. I'm sorry I didn't have time to talk - we had staff meetings until five and I could not be called away from them.

    Tyler is doing fine. He will read when he is ready, and probably not before. I am more concerned that he read when he is forty than that he read in the twelfth week of first grade. I am there to help him when he needs it, in what way I can.

    If you would like to talk to me, I suggest you come in on Tuesday, directly after school - I can keep Tyler in class when the buses leave. Please call the school to confirm, if you wish to come.

Yours,

Althea Elliot

From the first-grade teacher

From the desk of **Althea Elliot**

Dear Mrs. Bennet,

   I appreciate your observations. I know you are worried. Tyler is doing fine. He is performing exactly as expected at his grade level. It is normal for a child to confuse sounds at this age and also typical that he guess, rather than really read. We all guess, most of the time.
   If you would like to talk to me, please come in on Tuesday, directly after school.

Yours,

Althea Elliot

From the first-grade teacher

Dear Rhonda,

    Thank you so much for the beautiful soaps. They smell lovely. And thank you for the card. You are wrong; most of the work done was done by your son. I am glad to have had Tyler; he contributed very much to my class this year. He is a bright, strong student, and will do wonderfully in second grade. I have recommended that he have Mrs. Yount; she will provide the structure Tyler needs in order for him to do his best.

Sincerely,

Althea

From the second-grade teacher, Tara Blasingame

Parkside Elementary

Dear Mrs. Bennet,

Please forgive the letter. I tried to call and got your machine, and feel funny about leaving a long message. Sometimes I think better when I'm able to sit at the computer and write.

Don't worry about Tyler. He is so bright! He does have a hard time staying on task, but while it can drive you crazy, it's more of a sign of his interest in the world than anything else. I know - I'm like that myself.

This morning, Tyler came to class in tears but wouldn't tell me what it was about. Shortly after he arrived, he was called down to Mr. Kaplansky's office, and that sent Tyler into tears again. He said it wasn't his fault, and I told him to go on down and that Mr. Kaplansky probably wouldn't put him in the school prison. That got him to laugh!

It turns out that Tyler had a fight with Randall Turner on the bus. I know we have talked about Randall before. I talked with Tyler about it after lunch - he said that Randall insists on sitting with him on the bus, and then teases him. Tyler said he didn't know what to do, so finally he yelled and pushed him and then Randall hit him. I don't know the whole history, but at recess time, I pulled Tyler and Randall up against the slide and asked them what was going on. Randall fell apart! Randall is not in my class - he's in Selma Yount's class, but she says that although he talks a big game, he is really a pushover.

I'm telling you all of this because of what happened next. Randall started blubbering and there was a bunch of students around and they all started watching. I was thinking, "Oh, Tara, what did you do this for?", when all of a sudden, your Tyler put his hand on Randall's shoulder and said, "It's okay, Randall, I understand," and then he turned to all the other kids and said, "Everybody just leave us alone for a little while, okay?" I could have hugged him. What a guy.

Did you say you had some concerns about the math program? Please come see me.

Yours,

Tara

Tara Blasingame

216 Park Street · Viewcrest, MA 02772 · 508-555-1245

To the third-grade teacher, Roger Cunningham

Rhonda Bennet

Dear Mr. Cunningham,

Last night, Tyler's puppy was hit by a car and was killed. Tyler saw it happen. He is very upset. He insisted on coming to school. If he doesn't feel he can handle it, please call me at work, and I can make arrangements to pick him up. As you know, we only had the puppy for a month. We're all upset. I'm worse off than Tyler, I think.

Sincerely,

Rhonda Bennet

From the third-grade teacher

Dear Mrs. Bennet,

    I am sending Tyler home with a book, <u>The Tenth Good Thing About Barney</u>. I read it to my own children when our dog died. In circle today, Tyler told everyone what happened. The children said more than I could – losing pets is their favorite subject. Please call me if you think there is more that I can do. I am very sorry.

Roger Cunningham

From the fourth-grade teacher, Patricia Corning

 Parkside Elementary

Dear Mrs. Bennet,

   This is a follow-up to our conversation. I'm writing you to make sure I say what I mean. And since you were being honest with me, I'll be honest with you.
   I really am sorry that you have to spend time with Tyler on things you think he should have learned in school. We spent two sessions on the aspect of division that Tyler has struggled with. I try my best to keep track of who is having trouble with the basic concepts.
   If Tyler needs extra help, we can schedule a recess session. Unfortunately I only have so much time to cover material that's expected of us in preparation for the upcoming tests. If there were more time, or I was in more control of the curriculum, I promise you my approach would be different.
   As I said, I'll make time to talk to Tyler during recess. Any help you can give at home would be great. Thank you.

Yours,

Patricia Corning
Patricia Corning

Form letter from the fifth-grade teacher, David Tullock

Parkside Elementary School
Grade 5, room 203
Mr. Tullock

__November 16__
date

To the parents/guardians of __Tyler Bennet__,

Your (son)/daughter is:

__Having trouble completing his homework assignments on time.__

As his teacher, I am concerned about this and want him to succeed in class. Because I believe communication between school and home is an important part of the learning experience, I am writing to let you know of my concern. Attached are guidelines which were given to students at the beginning of the year. Please review them with your child to insure (he)/she understands their importance.

Please sign the letter below and have it returned to me at your earliest possible convenience.

Together, we can help insure that your child performs to the best of (his)/her ability.

Sincerely,

D. Tullock
David Tullock

I have read this letter and discussed the concern(s) with my child.

_____   _____
name   date

To the fifth-grade teacher

Rhonda Bennet

Dear Mr. Tullock,

I have enclosed the signed form as you requested. I am bothered that this is the first communication that I have had from you on this subject. When I talked to you about the field trip last month, you made no mention of Tyler's problem with homework. Has it only been in the past month that he has had trouble?

Tyler sometimes tunes out if he feels that he is not being challenged. I have spoken with him about his homework, and I intend to keep after him at home. What can we do to make sure that he is actively engaged at school?

I will call so that we can discuss this problem.

Sincerely yours,

Rhonda Bennet

To the second-grade teacher, Tara Blasingame

From:	**Rhonda Bennet <rhondabennet@email.com>**
Subject:	**Tyler Bennet**
To:	**Tara Blasingame <tblasingame@viewcrest.k12.ma.us>**

Dear Tara,

I wonder if you can help me. Tyler is in Mr. Tullock's class and not enjoying it. Mr. Tullock doesn't seem to be engaging Tyler and seems to think it is Tyler's attitude. I am not sure, since other than a form letter about his homework, Mr. Tullock hasn't said much. I tried to talk to him the other day, but he seemed to be in a hurry.

What do you think I should do? Have other students had problems? His lessons just don't seem very interesting to me. He's also gruff. Can you give me any suggestions? Tyler is miserable.

Thanks,

Rhonda

From the second-grade teacher

From:	Tara Blasingame <tblasingame@viewcrest.k12.ma.us>
Subject:	**Tyler Bennet**
To:	Rhonda Bennet <rhondabennet@email.com>

Dear Rhonda,

If you are having troubles with Mr. Tullock, I would go see Mr. Kaplansky. Tyler is a good student - he will be fine.

I'm wondering if Tyler might not like to come in and read to my second graders on Tuesday afternoons. I have been thinking about having some older students come in during the silent reading period to read their favorite books from second grade. Tyler would do a wonderful job. It would be towards the end of the day, and he could see if he liked it. I could speak to Mr. Tullock about it, too, if you wished.

Yours,

Tara

Tara Blasingame
Parkside Elementary School, Viewcrest MA
Grade 2

From the fifth-grade teacher

Parkside Elementary

Mrs. Bennet,

  Mr. Kaplansky told me about your meeting with him. I am sorry you missed me when you called. I will be in my classroom after school on Tuesday and Thursday this week until four o'clock.

Sincerely,

David Tullock

David Tullock

From the sixth-grade history teacher,
Daniel Sollenberg

DANIEL SOLLENBERG

Dear Mrs. Bennet,

    While I have written a note to Tyler, thanking him for the gift, I suspect I should thank you, too. The boxes of chocolates and tins of cookies other students have given are very nice and, unfortunately, I will probably eat all of them. So too, are the Christmas ornaments, if I can figure out where to hang them on Hannukah. But then, there is also the beautifully illustrated copy of <u>The Odyssey</u> in a wonderful new translation. For all of these gifts, I will write thank you notes, but I will have only one of them ten years from now. I'll think of Tyler every time I read about the wine-dark sea, which will be often. As you know, Homer is my favorite.

    Tyler is a joy to have in class. The walls are a putrid shade of green; the windows looking out to the parking lot are dirty, and maybe better that way, since I don't have to look at the parking lot; grading is a colossal bore; but I am reminded that there is always the chance, however slight, and almost seemingly by accident, that an incident may occur during the day which brings meaning to the world and to life. I get eight or ten of these a year - that is enough to keep me going, fool that I am. Tyler has given me at least three of these already, most recently when he leapt from his chair and said, "Some democracy in Greece! Hardly anybody could vote! What kind of democracy is that?" Most students stared at him blankly. A few giggled. One or two nodded. I could have kissed him, but I didn't want to embarrass him, and doing so might get me fired.

    I am sorry for the mix-up about your husband - I thought he wrote children's books. You're right - they would probably be bored hearing about themselves. Or maybe not - I always need to have a spare lesson in my pocket.

Faithfully yours,

Daniel Sollenberg
Daniel Sollenberg

From the eighth-grade English teacher,
Regina Harris

86 SCHOOL STREET
VIEWCREST, MASSACHUSETTS 02772
(508) 555-6849

Dear Mrs. Bennet,

  I need your help. Tyler is doing well in his work, but he frequently talks out of turn in class, and it's beginning to influence the rest of the students. I usually don't mind students speaking without raising hands, if it's related to the material, but unfortunately, Tyler's comments are usually meant to be funny and attract attention to him, not the subject. I have spoken to him about it (I don't know if he has mentioned that to you, though if he did, he wouldn't be like 99.9% of the eighth grade boys I know). He was better for a week or so, but it's started up again. Yesterday, I got angry - I told him I was going to talk to you. That quieted him down; it is probably enough, but I try to follow up my threats. Could you speak to him? I believe one sentence from you will do more than I can do, short of talking to the principal.
  Thanks.

Sincerely,

Regina Harris

Regina Harris

To the eighth-grade English teacher

From:	Rhonda Bennet <rhondabennet@email.com>
Subject:	**Thank You**
To:	Regina Harris <rharris@viewcrest.k12.ma.us>

Dear Ms. Harris,

Thanks for your note. I have spoken to Tyler. I told him if he misbehaves, we will ground him for life. (Just kidding.) He knows you know I know you know. Please call me if there are any further problems.

Sincerely,

Rhonda Bennet

P.S. Any suggestions about getting him to speak in anything other than monosyllables?

To the ninth-grade science teacher,
Theresa Ragins

Rhonda Bennet

Dear Mrs. Ragins,

I am writing to you with some apprehension, since I have encouraged Tyler to take care of himself in school. At fourteen, he should be able to do that. Right now he doesn't seem able to.

Tyler came home with the graded test from science yesterday and was beside himself. He is not used to failing. In spite of myself, I scolded him for not studying more. He didn't need that, probably, since he was beating himself up already. But Tyler indicated to me that the test was unfair and that it covered material not discussed in class. Then he said that he didn't like science anyway, and wasn't good at it.

I am not worried about a test score. I am worried that we are losing Tyler as a science student. I can assure him that he is capable, but to a fourteen year old, a mother's words seem to go in one ear and out the other. After all, what else would a mother say?

Two years ago, Tyler did wonderfully in science. His teacher, Mr. Watters, engaged him, and in fact, science was one of his best subjects. Last year, the teacher he had was, I think, disorganized and bored with the material. When Tyler didn't do his work, the teacher said little. And Tyler did little work. It was hard to help him, since the assignments seemed so vague.

Tyler comes to you ready to believe that science is not for him. My husband and I have tried to convince him otherwise, but we are not as effective as you could be.

Please forgive me: Let me tell you who I think my son is. Tyler is someone who, when challenged and treated maturely, responds with his best work. When he is not - because the material is not challenging, or the teacher seems uninterested and judgmental about who he is - he tunes out. Sometimes, we can get him to go along and make lemonade- sometimes we can't. I wish he weren't this way. He shouldn't be. But he is. I would like him to change, and maybe we can help him change. But I am most afraid that if someone doesn't reach out to him this year, he's going to give up on science.

I have told Tyler to talk to you. Could you please check in with him? Yes, I am his mother, but I can tell you, when he's good, he's very, very good. When he's bad, he's not much fun to be around. I'm sure you want the same thing I want - a good science student.

If there is something we can do, let me know.

Rhonda Bennet

From the eleventh-grade history teacher and advisor,
Dennis Turino

VIEWCREST HIGH SCHOOL
1345 Lakeside Hwy. • Viewcrest, Massachusetts 02772 • 508-555-7628

Dear Mrs. Bennet,

It was good to talk to you on the phone yesterday. Of course, while all of us at the school are a little lost about what to do in this kind of situation, we, as the grownups, still get to be in charge. It's hard to be in charge when you're a little lost yourself. The kids ask me questions that I have no answers for. And of course, the questions from someone like Tyler seem more important and challenging, since Brian was one of his closest friends.

I, too, have been very concerned about Tyler. He has been quiet with me and seemingly morose. Everyone walks on eggshells, since our jobs are no longer clear. After all, how important is the American system of government when you lose a friend? Not very. What are we really teaching anyway?

I would not be truthful if I did not tell you that when I was in eleventh grade my closest friend died in a motorcycle accident. It wasn't his fault. Even now, I can't explain it. And only now do I realize that I am still angry and confused by it. I don't feel qualified to teach about this, because I don't understand it myself. What could I say to Tyler? I did what I could, which is to tell him I know how it feels because it happened to me, too. Tyler only nodded. I was sure I didn't get through. But Tyler will be fine. I know that now, and I want to tell you why I know it.

As you know, there was a school assembly yesterday about Brian's death. While I went along with the idea, I now confess I was a little apprehensive about the whole thing. A group of students organized the assembly. They did a good job. As you probably know, Tyler was not one of them, although I encouraged him to be. I couldn't help but think that Tyler felt that everyone was pretending to have the pain that he felt. Maybe I am remembering how I felt when my friend died. No one else really understood. Sometimes, the solipsism of youth is correct.

I watched Tyler closely during the assembly. He sat close to the front, but didn't seem to be listening. School schedules being what they are, there were forty-two minutes for six hundred students to say how they felt. At fifty minutes, Mr. Taskin stood up and said it was time to go back to class, and that the sharing could go on during free periods; that was when Tyler stood up. He walked to the podium and stood there. I don't know what he said to Mr. Taskin, who can be pretty hard-nosed, but Mr. Taskin stood aside. I assume he knew that Tyler was Brian's close friend.

Tyler stood at the podium without speaking. And then, he cried. Mr. Taskin moved towards him, but Tyler held him off. He stood, crying. And while crying seems to be about losing control, it also seems it was what Tyler had planned to do. When he finished he talked briefly and eloquently about Brian, and about the hurt that he had and would carry with him from now on. He told us to value each other while we were here, living. And then, he walked over to Mr. Taskin, standing there awkwardly at the side of the stage, and he gave him a hug.

It was like a huge release for all of us. Without a word, just about everybody hugged somebody else. I am not much for hugs, but I hugged Mrs. Sandoval. And somehow, now I am not quite so hurt about Bobby Ryman, who died all those years ago.

We were all late for class.

You have a magnificent son.

Tyler will be fine.

Yours,

Dennis Turino

Dennis Turino

Tyler Bennet

• • •

Please join my parents and me
in celebrating my graduation from
high school
June 2
2:00pm
Viewcrest High School Auditorium

Party in our backyard at 4:00pm.

I needed all of you.

Tyler

To Theresa Ragins, science teacher

Rhonda Bennet

Dear Theresa,

   As you know, Tyler got in. We had decided it wasn't the most important thing in the world, but we breathed a huge sigh of relief and excitement when he got the letter. Tyler was much clearer about its relative importance than we were. He is much more philosophical than I am. He has always been that way. When he was in second grade, he understood the bully who was mean to him on the bus, while I felt like a mother bear who wanted to protect her cub.
   The credit goes mostly to Tyler, but let me tell you something I have been thinking. Tyler is there because of your recommendation. I feel sure of it. This doesn't mean that Tyler shouldn't go there - it only means that any number of students probably could go, but they chose Tyler, and it's because of you.
   When I read the copy of your letter, my breath caught. Could this be my son? It doesn't mention the call from the police last year. Or the failed math test in fifth grade. Or the way he treated his younger brother, only last week. What it did mention was the best of who Tyler is and the best that Tyler is able to become. For that, I am eternally grateful - for that and for the care you showed when he needed it most. In ninth grade, and this year in biology, you made him wonderful. Or maybe I should say you let him be wonderful. If he would only pick up his clothes and fill the gas tank.
   A long time ago, I read a book by Elie Wiesel called <u>Dawn</u>. In it, an Israeli soldier has a Palestinian soldier in a basement with orders to execute him at dawn if Israeli prisoners are not released. There in the twilight, unsure of what he should do, he sees every person he has ever known standing

in the room with him, waiting to see what he will do. They are waiting to see what he will do because they are all responsible for his choice. I have never been able to get that image out of my mind.

Now, only now, when my son is almost gone, do I realize that my son is all of us. He is me, and I am responsible for that, and he is his father, and grandparents, but he is also all of his teachers, and they have made him in ways I never could have. I have failed in so many ways that sometimes I wake at night and think, "Oh, no, I haven't taught him that. How can he make it? What can I do?" I will feel that until I die. But some of the things I never could have taught him, some places where I surely would have failed even if I had tried, you and others have accomplished. Whatever choices Tyler has to make, the better part of me believes that he will make the right ones, because of people like you.

Thank you. Thank you.

Yours,

Rhonda Bennet

Final Thoughts

The mother in these letters, Rhonda Bennet, is only one mother, and an imagined one at that. The way she negotiates her way through her son's education is not meant to be a prescription for any particular problem, but rather the suggestion of an approach – which is a continued attempt to communicate. Every child, every parent, every teacher is different, and so each has to find his or her own way, according to personality, place and predicament. The way in which we approach these relationships depends on who we are. This work of communicating, it seems to me, is more like a dance than a procedure – you learn the basic steps, and then respond to the partner.

What's the secret, though? That reminds me of a story.

When I first started telling stories, I was working at a branch library in a tough part of Providence, Rhode Island. Running an afternoon workshop for school-aged kids, nothing seemed to work – week after week, they threw books, fought with each other, and didn't listen to me; I had no idea what I was doing. Finally, at the end of my patience and ideas, I told the head librarian, Priscilla Harris, of my failure. "I don't know what to do," I told her. "They listen to you, but they won't listen to me."

Priscilla had been there a while and seen a lot of things – the library was as much a social service center as a place where one borrowed books. She smiled at me, nodded and said, "There's nothing I can tell you but to just keep talking and listening."

Those were frustrating words at the time, but now, years later, I see the wisdom in them. Oftentimes, there is no magic answer, no one right way – there is only the effort to keep communicating.

Here are some things I have learned in my own fumbling attempts at communicating:

- Some of the people you talk to will not hear you.
- Some of the people you listen to will not know you are listening.
- There is vulnerability in communicating.
- If you attempt to communicate, you will be hurt, and at times you will be sad.
- And, of course, you will be happy and you will be loved.

Also by Bill Harley

CDs and Books

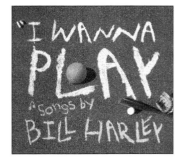

For a complete listing of Bill Harley's award-winning books and recordings or to schedule an appearance with Bill please visit: www.billharley.com or call 800-682-9522

Bill Harley

photo by Susan Wilson

Storyteller, musician, parent, educator and author, **Bill Harley** is a Grammy® award-winning artist who uses song and story to paint a vibrant picture of growing up, schooling and family life. Recipient of a 2010 Lifetime Achievement Award from the Rhode Island Council for the Humanities "for building community, promoting our common humanity, and encouraging lifelong learning, exploring and growing," Harley is also a long-time commentator for NPR's "All Things Considered". Bill tours nationwide as an author, performing artist and keynote speaker. He makes his home in Seekonk, MA with his wife Debbie Block, two beehives and a large dog. For more information please visit www.billharley.com or call 800-682-9522.

Additional resources and discussion questions available at:
www.billharley.com/betweenhomeandschool.asp

Made in the USA
Charleston, SC
24 September 2010

Praise for Between Home and School

"I love this lovely little book. I laughed and cried a[...] and teachers as they worked together to mentor t[...]
— *Amy Dickinson,* BESTSELLING AUTHOR OF *THE M[...]*
CHICAGO TRIBUNE - SYNDICATED COLUMNIST "ASK AM[...]

"If more of us from all sides of the home a[nd school] approach things with Bill's perspective, our kids w[...]. *Between Home and School* provides a simple and beautiful example of a Mom and her son's teachers collaborating for long-term school success."
— *Tim Sullivan,* FOUNDER, SCHOOL FAMILY MEDIA AND PTO TODAY

"In this imagined exchange of letters between a mother and her son's teachers, nary a finger is wagged, nor a line drawn in the sand. Harley's keen understanding of the promise and possibility of clear and careful communication should be a lesson to us all."
— *Claire Green,* PRESIDENT, PARENTS' CHOICE FOUNDATION

"Clearly Bill Harley knows kids, teachers and the joys of parenting. What appears as a simple correspondence between a mom and her son's teachers ultimately elicits thoughtful reflections on a key relationship in a child's life: that of parent-child-teacher."
— *Barbara Smith Decker,* NATIONAL PARENTING PUBLICATIONS AWARD (NAPPA) MANAGER

"Readers will appreciate something we all need to be reminded of: home affects school affects home...There is a person and a life behind the roles of parent, student and teacher. Harley's observations are 'spot on'."
— *Greg Weiss,* DRAMA & SPEECH TEACHER, JAMES HART & MILLENNIUM SCHOOLS (GRADES 5 - 8), HOMEWOOD, IL; STORYTELLER; AUTHOR

Book design by Alison Tolman-Rogers

©2010
All Rights Reserved
ROUND RIVER PRODUCTIONS
301 Jacob Street
Seekonk, MA 02771
800-682-9522
www.billharley.com

$8.00
ISBN 978-1-878126-56-6